ECDL3

for Microsoft Office 2000

Brendan Munnelly and Paul Holden

Using a Computer and Managing Files

*Everything you need to pass the European
Computer Driving Licence, module by module*

Prentice
Hall

An imprint of Pearson Education

London · New York · Sydney · Tokyo · Singapore ·
Madrid · Mexico City · Munich · Paris

PEARSON EDUCATION LIMITED

Head Office:
Edinburgh Gate
Harlow CM20 2JE
Tel: +44 (0)1279 623623
Fax: +44 (0)1279 431059

London Office:
128 Long Acre
London WC2E 9AN
Tel: +44 (0)20 7447 2000
Fax: +44 (0)20 7240 5771

Website: www.it-minds.com

This edition published in Great Britain in 2002

First published in Great Britain in 2002 as part of
ECDL3 The Complete Coursebook for Microsoft Office 2000

© Rédacteurs Limited 2002

ISBN 0-130-35459-7

British Library Cataloguing in Publication Data
A CIP catalogue record for this book can be obtained from the British Library

'European Computer Driving Licence' and ECDL and Stars device are registered trademarks of the European Computer Driving Licence Foundation Limited. Rédacteurs Limited is an independent entity from the European Computer Driving Licence Foundation Limited, and not affiliated with the European Computer Driving Licence Foundation in any manner.

This book may be used in assisting students to prepare for the European Computer Driving Licence Examination. Neither the European Computer Driving Licence Foundation Limited, Rédacteurs Limited nor the publisher warrants that the use of this book will ensure passing the relevant examination.

Use of the ECDL-F approved Courseware logo on this product signifies that it has been independently reviewed and approved in complying with the following standards:

Acceptable coverage of all courseware content related to ECDL syllabus Module 2 version 3.0. This courseware material has not been reviewed for technical accuracy and does not guarantee that the end user will pass the associated ECDL examinations. Any and all assessment tests and/or performance based exercises contained in these Modular books relate solely to these books and do not constitute, or imply, certification by the European Driving Licence Foundation in respect of any ECDL examinations. For details on sitting ECDL examinations in your country please contact the local ECDL licensee or visit the European Computer Driving Licence Foundation Limited web site at http://www.ecdl.com.

References to the European Computer Driving Licence (ECDL) include the International Computer Driving Licence (ICDL).

ECDL Foundation Syllabus Version 3.0 is published as the official syllabus for use within the European Computer Driving Licence (ECDL) and International Computer Driving Licence (ICDL) certification programmes.

Rédacteurs Limited is at http://www.redact.ie

Brendan Munnelly is at http://www.munnelly.com

10 9 8 7 6 5 4 3 2 1

Typeset by Pantek Arts, Maidstone, Kent.
Printed and bound in Great Britain by Ashford Colour Press, Gosport, Hampshire.

The Publishers' policy is to use paper manufactured from sustainable forests.

Preface

The European Computer Driving Licence (ECDL) is an internationally recognized qualification in end-user computer skills. It is designed to give employers and job-seekers a standard against which they can measure competence – not in theory, but in practice. Its seven Modules cover the areas most frequently required in today's business environment. More than one million people in over fifty countries have undertaken ECDL in order to benefit from the personal, social and business advantages and international mobility that it provides.

In addition to its application in business, the ECDL has a social and cultural purpose. With the proliferation of computers into every aspect of modern life, there is a danger that society will break down into two groups – the information 'haves' and the information 'have nots'. The seven modules of the ECDL are not difficult, but they equip anyone who passes them to participate actively and fully in the Information Society.

The ECDL is not product-specific – you can use any hardware or software to perform the tasks in the examinations. And you can take the seven examinations in any order, and work through the syllabus at your own pace.

This book is one of a set of seven, each dealing with one of the ECDL modules. While each book can be used independently, we recommend that you read this one, *Using a Computer and Managing Files*, before reading any of the other practical modules (3 to 7). This module teaches you the basic operations that are needed in the other practical modules.

The examples in these books are based on PCs (rather than Apple Macintoshes), and on Microsoft software, as follows:

- Operating system: Microsoft Windows 95/98
- Word Processing: Microsoft Word 2000
- Spreadsheets: Microsoft Excel 2000
- Databases: Microsoft Access 2000
- Presentations: Microsoft PowerPoint 2000
- Information and Communication: Microsoft Internet Explorer 5.0 and Microsoft Outlook Express 5.0

If you use other hardware or software, you can use the principles discussed in this book, but the details of operation will differ.

Welcome to the world of computers!

CONTENTS

Introduction

In this ECDL Module, you get to meet the natives of computer land in the flesh.

And what exotic creatures they are! The citizens are called files. They reside in houses called folders. And folders are built on areas called drives. (Files inside folders, and folders on top of drives – you have learnt quite a lot already!)

And such obedient citizens too! You can change their names, move them to a different location, alter their appearance, get rid of ones you don't want anymore – you can even create new ones out of nothing.

But remember this: files are delicate. So treat them with care. You do this by saving them regularly and by making copies of them every so often – just in case something bad happens to the originals. It's always the files you like and need most that seem to disappear the quickest. It's better to learn this lesson from a book than from a real-life mishap in computer land.

CHAPTER 1

Starting up, clicking around, shutting down

In this chapter

Are you ready to take your first practical steps in computing? This chapter guides you through the basics. You will learn the correct ways of starting and shutting down a computer, discover the meaning of the various little pictures on the Windows screen, and find out how to start and close Word, Excel, and other software applications that you will meet in later ECDL modules.

New skills

At the end of this chapter you should be able to:
- Power up and power down a computer
- Use the Start menu to open software applications
- Switch between open applications

- Click, double-click, right-click, and drag with the mouse
- Use the three control buttons at the top right of a window
- Move, resize, and scroll windows
- Restart a computer when problems occur

New words

At the end of this chapter you should be able to explain the following terms:

- Powering up/Booting
- Cursor
- Clicking
- Menu
- Taskbar
- Close button
- Restore button
- Folder

- Desktop window
- Application window
- Maximize button
- Minimize button
- Dragging
- Double-clicking
- Pop-up/Shortcut menu
- Dialog box

Starting your computer

Before you start your computer, check that it is plugged into the electricity socket. Now, press the button to switch on the computer.

- On some computers, a *single button* switches on both the computer and the computer's screen.

- Other computers have *two buttons*: one for the computer itself and a second for the screen.

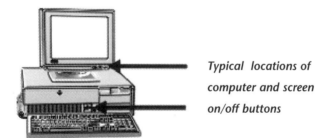

Typical locations of computer and screen on/off buttons

Your computer will make some humming noises and some messages will flicker on your screen. Don't worry: this is just your computer warming up and checking that everything is in working order.

The Windows desktop

The Windows desktop appears – little pictures set against a coloured background. These pictures are called *icons*. Along the bottom of your screen you will see a grey bar, with a button named Start in its left corner and a clock in its right. This is called the *taskbar*.

   You will learn more about icons and the taskbar later. You will also discover how you can change the appearance of your Windows desktop to suit your working needs and personal taste.

A sample Windows desktop. The little pictures are called icons.
The grey bar along the bottom of the screen is called the taskbar.

Congratulations. You have now powered up your computer.

Powering up/booting

The technical terms for starting a computer and displaying the Windows desktop on the screen. You don't 'switch on' a computer; you 'power it up' or 'boot' it.

Starting applications

Software applications are useful programs such as Microsoft Word, Excel, Access, and PowerPoint that enable you to create documents, spreadsheets, databases and presentations. You will learn a lot about these in Modules 3, 4, 5, and 6 of this ECDL course. Your first step in working with applications is to learn how to start them.

Using the mouse

Place your hand over the mouse and move it around your (physical) desktop. As you move the mouse, the cursor moves around the Windows desktop, allowing you to point to the item you want to work with.

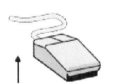 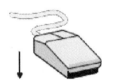

To move the cursor up the screen, move the mouse in the up direction.

To move the cursor down the screen, move the mouse in the down direction.

Cursor

A symbol, usually an arrow, that you move around the computer screen by moving the mouse across your (physical) desktop.

The Start button

Move the cursor down to the bottom-left of
your screen so that it is over the **Start** button.
Now, press down the left mouse button and then release it.
You don't need to hold down the button for more than a
second. This is called clicking.

Clicking with the mouse

*Briefly holding down the left mouse button. By clicking on
an item on the screen, you tell your computer: 'I want to
select this item'.*

Windows start-up menu

Your mouse-click causes the **Start**
button to display the start-up
menu. Move the cursor up over
the item called **Programs**. As you
do, another menu appears to its
right. On this second menu, or
submenu, move the cursor over
the item called **Microsoft Word**
and click on it. This opens the
Microsoft Word application.

Menu

*A list of items displayed on the computer screen that allows
you to work with applications and files, and get more
information. Some menus offer submenus of further options.*

Multi-tasking with Windows

You can open more than one application at one time – this is called multi-tasking. Move the cursor back down over the **Start** button and click on it. Next, move the cursor over the menu item called **Programs**. On the next menu displayed, move the cursor over the item called **Microsoft Excel** and click on it. You have now started a second application.

Why stop at two applications? Exercise 1.1 takes you through the steps of starting a third application, Notepad.

Exercise 1.1: Opening the Notepad application

1 Click on the **Start** button.

2 Click **Start | Programs** to display the start-up menu.

3 Click **Start | Programs | Accessories** to display the Accessories submenu.

4 Click **Start | Programs | Accessories | Notepad** to open the Notepad application.

   Congratulations. You have now three applications open on your screen.

The expression **Start | Programs** is a shorthand way of saying 'Open the start-up menu and select the option named Programs'. And **Start | Programs | Accessories | Notepad** means: 'Open the start-up menu and select the option called Programs. Next, on the Programs menu, choose the option named Accessories, and on the Accessories menu, choose Notepad'.

   Although you can have lots of applications open at one time, only one can be in the foreground; the others wait behind it in the background. How do you tell Windows which application you want to bring to the foreground?

Take a look at the taskbar along the bottom of your Windows desktop. Notice how it displays the names of all your open applications.

Click on an application's name to display it in the foreground

To select one, for example, Notepad, click on Notepad. Or, to select Excel, click on Excel. You use the taskbar to switch between open applications and display a particular one in the foreground.

Taskbar

> *A horizontal bar across the bottom of the Windows desktop that displays the Start button, plus the names of any open applications. Click an application's name to display it in the foreground.*

You will find Windows' ability to open several applications at one time very useful. For example, you could have the following open on your computer: a Word letter (see Module 3), an Excel spreadsheet (Module 4), and an e-mail (Module 7). As you will also learn, you can copy items from one application to another.

Multi-tasking

> *The ability of Windows to open several applications and files at one time.*

The control buttons

Using the taskbar, switch to Notepad. Notice the three buttons at the top-right? These are called *control buttons*. You can use these to perform various actions, as the following exercises show.

Exercise 1.2: Using the Close button to close a Notepad

1 Is Notepad in the foreground? If not, click its name on the taskbar.

Close button

2 Move the mouse to the top-right of the Notepad screen, and click on the button that contains an X.

You have closed the Notepad application by clicking on one of the control buttons – the Close button.

Close button
> *A button at the top right of an application window that, if selected, closes the application.*

In the next two exercises you will learn how to use the Restore and Maximize control buttons.

Exercise 1.3: Using the Restore button to reduce a Window's size

1 Is Excel in the foreground? If not, click its name on the taskbar.

2   Move the mouse to the top-right of the Excel
screen, and click on the Restore button.

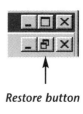

This reduces the size of the Excel screen,
so that it no longer fills the entire
Windows desktop.

Restore button

3   Using the taskbar, switch to Word. Click on Word's
Restore button.

You should now be able to see both applications on your
screen, with the currently selected application (Word)
overlapping the other (Excel). Each application appears
within its own *window*.

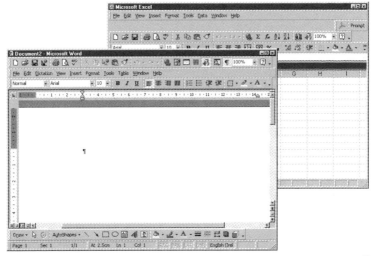

Overlapping application windows of Microsoft Word and Microsoft Excel

Restore button

> *A button beside the Close button that reduces the size of
> the application screen area.*

To bring Excel to the foreground, click on any part of its window. You do not need to click its name on the taskbar. The Excel window now overlaps the Word window. To return the Word window to the foreground, click on any part of it.

Application window

A rectangular area that can display a file or files from an application. All application windows, regardless of their content, share common components and features.

When you click on a Restore button to reduce the size of a window, the Restore button disappears and is replaced by another button, called the Maximize button.

Maximize button

Clicking on this button reverses the effect of Restore: that is, it increases the size of the window so that it again fills the Windows desktop.

Maximize button

A button that increases the size of a previously reduced window so that it fills the entire Windows desktop.

One control button remains: the Minimize button. Exercise 1.4 provides an example of the Minimize button in use.

Minimize button

Exercise 1.4: Shrinking a window with the Minimize button

1   Is Word in the foreground? If not, click on any part of its window.

2 Click on Word's Minimize button.

This 'shrinks' Word so that it appears on the taskbar and nowhere else.

3 Click on any part of the Excel window to select it, and then click its Minimize button.

Both applications now appear only on the taskbar.

To display Word and Excel again, click on their names on the taskbar.

Minimize button

A button that shrinks an application window to remove it from the desktop to the taskbar only.

You will find the Close, Restore or Maximize, and Minimize buttons at the top-right corner of every window.

Moving windows with the title bar

Another feature that every window shares is a title bar – the identifying bar that runs across the top of the window. You use the title bar to move a window to a different position on the desktop as follows:

- Click on the window's title bar – but do not release the mouse button.

- With your finger still on the mouse button, move the mouse to reposition the window.

- When you have positioned the window where you want it, release the mouse button.

Click on the title bar and drag to reposition a window

This series of click-move-release actions is called dragging.

Dragging with the mouse

Moving a selected item on the desktop by clicking on it with the left mouse button, and holding down the button as you move the item.

Using the Close button, close Excel. You now have only the Word application open on your desktop.

Working with desktop windows

On the Windows desktop, move your cursor over the icon (little picture) named My Computer and click. Notice that the icon is highlighted. Your single-click selects it – but does not perform any action on it.

Now, click anywhere on the desktop to deselect the My Computer icon.

Once again, move the cursor over the My Computer icon. Now, click once and then, very quickly, click a second time on My Computer. This two-click action (called *double-clicking*) opens the My Computer icon so that you can see its contents.

A sample My Computer desktop window

Double-clicking with the mouse

To tell Windows to perform an action on a selected item,
press the left mouse button quickly twice in succession.

Click on the close box at the top-right of the My Computer
window to close it. My Computer is an example of a
desktop folder – an icon that represents a number of items
grouped together.

Except for My Computer,
every other folder on your
desktop looks like a 'real'
folder. Here are some examples.

Folder

An icon on the Windows desktop that contains within it
one or more icons representing applications, files, or
physical devices.

A window opened when a folder is double-clicked is called a desktop window. Desktop windows look like and can be used in a similar way to applications windows – so much so that the term 'window' is commonly used to describe either type.

Desktop window

> *A window opened when a folder is double-clicked.*
> *Desktop windows contain similar components and*
> *features to application windows.*

Practise opening folders on your desktop by double-clicking on them. Some folders, you may find, contain sub-folders. (A sub-folder is no different from a folder; it's just a folder that happens to be inside another folder.) Close any folder you open by using its close box.

Changing the shape and size of a window

You can change the shape and size of an application or desktop window by selecting it, and dragging any of its four sides.

To change the width of a window, click on its left or right edge. The cursor changes to a double-headed arrow. Then drag with the mouse. As you drag the window, its edges change to dashed lines.

To make a window taller or shorter, click on its top or bottom edge. Again, the cursor changes to a double-headed arrow. Drag the edge with the mouse.

To change both window height and width, click
in the bottom-right corner of the window. The
cursor changes to a double-headed, diagonal arrow.
Drag the corner with the mouse.

Practise your window resizing skills with the My Computer
folder window.

Scrolling a window

Sometimes a window may not be large enough to display all
its contents. In such cases, scroll bars appear on the right
and/or along the bottom of the window. To view a different
part of the window:

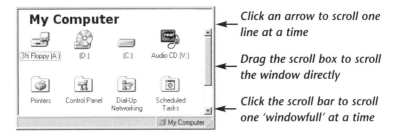

*Click an arrow to scroll one
line at a time*

*Drag the scroll box to scroll
the window directly*

*Click the scroll bar to scroll
one 'windowfull' at a time*

- The *position* of the scroll box in relation to the scroll
  bar indicates which area of the window you are
  viewing. When the scroll box is in the middle of the
  scroll bar, for example, the window is positioned
  halfway through its contents.

- The *size* of the scroll box indicates how much of the
  window's contents you can see at one time. For
  example, if the scroll box is half the length of the scroll
  bar, you can see half the contents.

Right-clicking and pop-up menus

In addition to clicking (to select), dragging (to move), and double-clicking (to perform an action), Windows offers a fourth kind of mouse movement: right-clicking.

To right-click something is to click on it once with the right mouse button.

Right-clicking on anything – whether a folder, application or file icon, or even the desktop – displays a pop-up menu. The menu options shown depend on the item you right-click.

Right-Clicking with the mouse

Briefly holding down the right mouse button. Windows responds by displaying a pop-up menu of options.

One option that a right-click always displays is called **Properties**. Select this option from the pop-up menu to view details about the item.

Practise right-clicking on icons and on the desktop background. In each case, click the **Properties** option on the pop-up menu.

Pop-up or shortcut menu

A small menu that appears temporarily, typically when you right-click on an item. When you select an option from a pop-up menu, the menu usually disappears.

Shutting down

The opposite of powering up a computer is powering or shutting it down. Never just switch off your computer – you may lose unsaved information and damage your computer's hard disk drive (thereby losing saved information too!)

To shut down your computer properly, follow the steps in Exercise 1.5:

Exercise 1.5: Shutting down your computer

1 Click the **Start** button.

2 Click **Shut Down**.

3 Select the Shut down option by clicking on it.

4 Click the **OK** button.

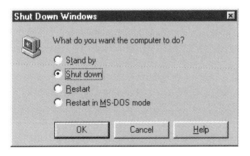

Some computers can switch themselves off automatically. On others, you need to press the on/off button after you see the message: 'It is now safe to turn off your computer'.

Now, power up your computer again – *but wait at least twenty seconds*. Otherwise, you may damage your computer's hard disk drive.

Restarting your computer

The Restart option has the same effect as powering down the computer and powering it up again very quickly – but without the risk of damage to the computer hardware.

Exercise 1.6: Restarting your computer

1 Click **Start | Shut Down**.

2 Select the Restart option, and click **OK**.

When your computer hangs

Sometimes, an application open on a computer may 'hang' or 'freeze'. This means that it does not respond to the pressing of any keys or any clicking with the mouse. On other occasions, Windows itself may fail to respond to any user action, with the result that the entire computer hangs. What do you do? This part provides the answers.

Application problems

When a particular application fails to respond to any action you take, press the following three keys simultaneously: Ctrl, Alt and Delete. Most computer users do this by holding down the Ctrl and Alt keys with the fingers of their left hand, and then pressing the Delete key with a finger of their right.

The shorthand way of writing 'Press the Ctrl, Alt and Delete keys simultaneously' is Ctrl+Alt+Delete.

You are then shown a window similar to the one below, which lists all the applications currently open on your computer. The frozen application is indicated by the message 'Not Responding'.

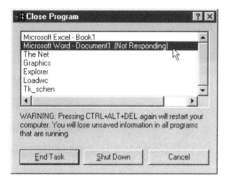

The Close Program dialog box showing a 'Not Responding' application

Click on the frozen application, and then click on the **End Task** button. The application closes, as does the Close Program window. You can then reopen the application in the usual way.

Windows problems

If Windows hangs and your computer freezes, press Ctrl+Alt+Delete *twice* in quick succession. This has the effect of powering down the computer and powering it up again very quickly – but without the risk of damage to the computer hardware. In fact, it has the same effect as selecting the Restart option from the Shut Down Windows window.

Improper shutdowns and ScanDisk

If you power down your computer in any way other than using **Start | Shut Down**, Windows will typically suggest that you run a program called ScanDisk when you next power up the computer. This checks your hard disk drive(s) for errors. Windows starts when ScanDisk finishes.

Dialog boxes

The Close Program window described in the previous topic is an example of a Windows *dialog box*. You will meet many such dialog boxes when you use Windows Explorer, Word, Excel and other applications.

Dialog box

> *A rectangular box that Windows displays when it needs further information before it can carry out a command, or when it needs to provide you with more information.*

Dialog box components

Dialog boxes typically contain some or all of the following components:

- **Command button**: A button that performs or cancels an action. OK and Cancel are the two most common buttons. Here are some more:

- **Drop-down list box**: A list of options that you can select from. Click the arrow on its right to view all the choices available.

The example below is from the Print dialog box. It shows the printer choices available to you. You click to select the one you require.

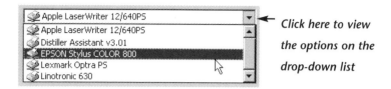

Click here to view the options on the drop-down list

- **Option buttons**: A group of *round buttons* indicating alternative choices. The example below is also from the Print dialog box.

- **Checkboxes**: A set of *square boxes* you can select or deselect to turn options on or off. More than one checkbox can be selected at one time.

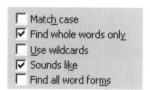

Default options

Most dialog boxes offer preselected or default settings. Unless you choose otherwise, the default settings decide which options and actions are performed. When you choose **Start | Shut Down**, for example, the default option is **Shut down**. To accept the defaults offered by a dialog box, simply press the Enter key.

Chapter summary: so now you know

To power up a computer, switch on the system box. If the screen has a separate on/off switch, switch it on also. Windows starts and displays icons on the *desktop*.

Use the **Start | Programs** menu to start software applications such as Word or Excel, and the *taskbar* to switch between open applications.

The *control buttons* at the top left of a window enable you to *restore* (decrease the size of), *maximize, minimize* and *close* that window. To *move* a window across the desktop, drag it by its *title bar*. To resize a window, drag its edges.

Icons on the desktop represent drives, applications, files and folders.

Clicking an item selects it. *Double-clicking* performs an action on it. And *right-clicking* displays a small, *pop-up menu* of relevant options.

Where a window is too small to display all its contents, *scroll* to view different parts of that window. When Windows needs further information before carrying out an action, it displays a *dialog box*.

Always use the *shut down* procedure when switching off your computer. To restart a 'hung' application, press Ctrl+Alt+Delete. Press the three keys twice in quick succession if Windows itself hangs.

CHAPTER 2

Exploring your computer

In this chapter

Ever wondered what information was stored on your computer? Or on someone else's computer? After reading this chapter, you will be able to answer such questions as: what drives are installed on a computer, what are the names of its folders and files, and what processor chip and how much memory does it have?

You will also discover how to find a particular file without knowing its name, and how to use the Windows online help system.

New skills

At the end of this chapter you should be able to:

- Distinguish between files, folders, and drives
- Use My Computer to view drives, folders, and files
- Change the order in which folders and files are displayed in My Computer

- View information about your computer's operating system, processor type, and amount of RAM
- Explain file name extensions and recognize the most common types
- Search for folders and files
- Use Windows online help

New words

At the end of this chapter you should be able to explain the following terms:

- File
- Subfolder
- My Computer
- File name extension
- Wildcard
- Folder
- Drive
- Recycle Bin
- Windows Find

How your computer stores information

If you throw all your belongings in a heap together on the floor, you will have a difficult time finding anything. How much easier to sort your valuables beforehand, dividing them neatly between shelves or drawers. When you need to find something, you know exactly where it is.

As with your belongings, so with information stored on a computer. In this chapter you will learn about files, folder and drives – the three levels at which information is organized on a computer.

Files

All the information and applications on your computer are stored in individual files. Think of a file as the computer's basic unit of storage.

File

The computer's basic unit of information storage. Everything on a computer is stored in a file of one type or another.

Folders

A computer may contain many thousands of files. To make it easier for you (and the computer) to find and keep track of files, you can group files together in folders.

Folder

A group of files. Files grouped into folders are easier to find and work with.

A folder can also contain one or more folders, thereby forming a tree-like hierarchy.

Sub-folder

A folder located within another folder.

A sample hierarchy of folders and files

In the example above, the folder named Word Documents contains two sub-folders: Letters and Reports.

Another advantage of placing files in a folder or sub-folder is that you can work with the files as a group. For example, you can copy or delete all files in a folder in a single operation.

Drives

A drive is a device that stores folders and files. Typical PCs have a hard disk drive that is named the C: drive. On some computers, the hard disk is divided ('partitioned') into two – a C: drive and a D: drive.

The next available letter after the hard disk is given to the CD-ROM drive. This can be D: or E:, depending on whether your hard drive is partitioned or not. The floppy diskette drive is named the A: drive.

Drive

A physical storage device for holding files and folders. Typically, A: is the floppy diskette drive, C: the hard disk, and D: is the CD-ROM drive.

Where is the B: drive? Early personal computers had just two floppy diskette drives, A: and B:. The advent of hard disks, which were named as C: drives, eliminated the need for a second floppy drive.

Using My Computer

Take a look at your Windows desktop. Can you see a folder named My Computer? If not, resize or minimize any open windows until the My Computer icon is visible.

My Computer

My Computer displays icons showing the hard disk, floppy diskette and CD-ROM drives on your PC. You can also see folders called Control Panel (in which you can change your computer's settings), Printers (for changing printer's settings) and Dial-up Networking (for changing internet connection settings).

My Computer

A desktop folder in which you view almost everything on your computer, including drive contents, and computer, printer and internet settings.

Exploring drives with My Computer

What disk drives does your computer contain? Find out in Exercise 2.1.

Exercise 2.1: Exploring drives with My Computer

1 Double-click the My Computer icon on the Windows desktop. In the example below, you can see four drives: a floppy diskette drive (A:), one hard disk drive (C:), and two CD-ROM drives (D: and V:).

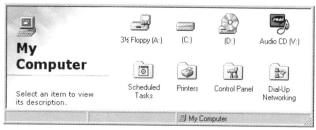

My Computer folder showing four drives

What drives are on your computer?

Now you know how to discover what drives are installed on your PC – or on any other PC you encounter. In Exercise 2.2, you will learn how to view basic information about an installed drive.

Exercise 2.2: Viewing Drive Properties

1 With the My Computer window open, right-click on the C: drive icon.

2 On the pop-up menu displayed, click the last option, **Properties**.

You are now shown a dialog box similar to the one on the right.

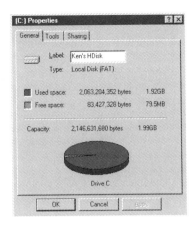

You can see how much space is occupied on your hard disk, and how much is still free. You can also use this dialog box to give a name ('label') to your hard disk drive.

3   When finished, click **OK**.

As further practice, perform this exercise on your other drives.

Leave the My Computer window open on your desktop. Note that an icon for the My Computer window is displayed on your taskbar.

Exploring folders and files with My Computer

You can use My Computer to display the folders and files contained on any drive of your computer. Just double-click a drive icon – for example, the C: icon – and My Computer opens a second window showing the selected drive's contents.

My Computer can display folders and files within a drive in a number of ways. Click the **View** menu to display the options available. Here are the main ones:

- **Large icons**: Displays folders and files like this:

- **Small icons**: Displays folders and files in columns, with folders at the top of each column and files underneath.

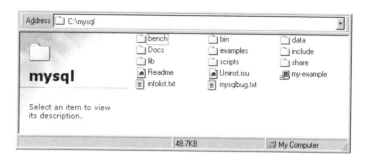

- **List**: Displays folders and files in columns, but lists all your folders before it shows the files.

- **Details**: Lists folders first and then files in a single column, and displays additional information about each item.

For the exercises in this book, choose **View | Details**. This viewing option provides the most information about your drives' contents.

Along the bottom of the My Computer window, in the Status Bar, you can see the number of items in the window, and the disk space that they occupy. Can't see the Status Bar or Toolbar? Click the relevant options on the View menu to display them.

Sorting folders and files

You can change the order in which My Computer displays your folders and files. By default, folders and files are listed alphabetically by name. To view them in order of size, for example, click on Size in the bar across the top of the window. Alternatively, you can sort them by Type or (date) Modified.

Exercise 2.3: Sorting Folders and Files in My Computer

1   Use My Computer to display the contents of your C: drive.

2   Click on Name in the window heading. My Computer sorts the folders and files in reverse alphabetical order. Click again on Name to re-sort them in their original order.

Name	Size	Type
zappkif.zip	155KB	WinZip File
ymsgr.exe	1,374KB	Application
ws_ftple.exe	691KB	Application

3   Click on Size in the window heading. My Computer sorts the folders and files in order of decreasing size, with the largest shown first. Click again on Size to resort them so that the smallest files are listed first.

4   Click on Modified in the window heading. My Computer sorts the folders and files so that the most recently created or changed are shown first. Click again on Modified to resort them so that the oldest are listed first.

You can make any column narrower or wider by clicking on the boundary line and holding down the mouse button. The cursor changes to a cross-hair. Next, drag the boundary left or right.

Looking at a folder's properties

To display information about a folder in My Computer – for example, the Windows folder – right-click on it. From the pop-up menu displayed, click the **Properties** option.

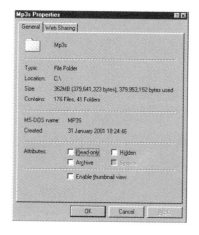

You are shown a dialog box similar to the one on the right.

Among other details, this tells you the number of folders and files within the folder.

It also shows the drive where the folder is located (in this case, C:), and the size of the folder (in this case, 362 megabytes).

File name extensions and icons

A file, as stated at the beginning of this chapter, is the basic unit of information storage on a computer. When you look at files in My Computer windows, you can see that different files are represented by different icons.

The icon that Windows uses to represent a file depends on the file's three-letter *file name extension*. Application files have

the extension .exe or .dll. A file name extension is separated
from the remainder of the file name by a full stop.

When you name and save a file within an application (for
example, a Word document within Microsoft Word),
Windows automatically attaches the appropriate three-letter
extension to that file.

File name extension

*A three-letter addition to a file name that indicates the
type of information stored in the file. A full stop separates
the extension from the remainder of the file name.*

Here are some common application file name extensions and
their icons:

Application File Type	Extension	Icon
Microsoft Word document	.doc	
Microsoft Excel spreadsheet	.xls	
Microsoft Access database	.mdb	
Microsoft PowerPoint presentation	.ppt	
Plain text file	.txt	
Online help file	.hlp	
Web page file	.htm	

Searching for folders and files

The quickest way to locate a folder or file on your (or anyone
else's) computer is to use the Windows Find feature. Most
Find actions are based on all or part of the folder or file name.
But Find also allows you perform sophisticated searches based
on date ranges or content.

To find a folder or file on a drive, choose the **Start | Find | Files or Folders** command. This displays the dialog box below. Using the Look in: box, you can specify My Computer (all your drives), a particular drive or a folder within a drive. In the Named: box, type the file name. Next, click **Find Now**.

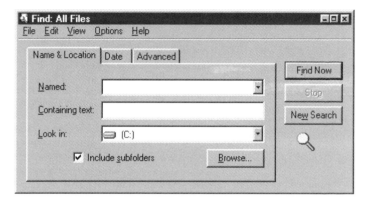

You can use the Browse button to display a My Computer-style view of the drives, folders, and files of the computer that you are searching on.

Wildcard searches

In folder and file names, an asterisk (*) is called a wildcard – it can represent one or several characters. If you cannot remember the full name of the item you want to search for, type the wildcard character in place of the missing letter(s).

For instance, report*.doc finds all files that begin with 'report' and have the .doc extension. Examples might be report3.doc, reportnew.doc and report-a.doc.

If you search for *.xls, Windows finds all files on your computer that have the Microsoft Excel file name extension. Try it and see!

Wildcard

An asterisk symbol (*) that can stand for one or a combination of characters when performing a search for a folder or file.

Exercise 2.3: Finding all Word documents using a wildcard

1 Choose **Start | Find | Files or Folders.**

2 In the Named: box, type *.doc.

3 In the Look in: box, select the C: drive.

4 Click **Find Now.**

   Windows displays all files ending in .doc in a My Computer-style window. You can open any listed file by double-clicking on it. To close the Find dialog box, click the Close button in the top-right corner.

Date-based searches

If you click on the Date Modified tab of the File Find dialog box, you can limit your search to only those folders or files created or changed between certain dates, or during a specified number of days or months.

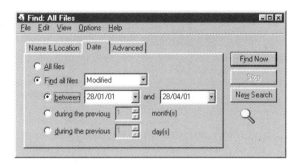

Limiting your search by date

You can search by date or date range alone, if you don't know the file or folder name. Or if you just want to see what folders or files were created or modified on or between certain dates.

Content-based searches

If you have absolutely no idea of the name of the item that you are looking for, or when it was created or modified, you can search by content.

Click on the Name & Location tab of the File Find dialog box and type one or more words you think are contained within the files you are searching for.

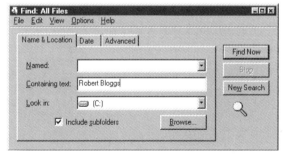

Searching by file content

Windows Find

> *A search feature that enables you to locate folders or files on any of the following bases: all or part of their name, date of creation or last modification, or their content.*

The Recycle Bin

Windows stores files that you delete in an area it calls the Recycle Bin. Can you see its icon on your Windows desktop? If not, resize or minimize some open windows.

Recycle Bin

Bin containing files marked for deletion

Recycle Bin

Empty bin

If you delete a file in error, double-click on the Recycle Bin icon, click the file to select it, and choose **File | Restore**. You can empty your Recycle Bin by choosing **File | Empty Recycle Bin**. Emptying your bin increases the free space available on your C: drive.

Recycle Bin

> *A storage area where Windows holds deleted files. You can retrieve items that you deleted in error, or empty the bin to free more disk space.*

Viewing your system information

What are your computer's specifications? To find out, follow these steps:

- Choose **Start | Settings | Control Panel** to display the Control Panel desktop folder.

- Alternatively, double-click the Control Panel icon within My Computer.

- Double-click the System icon.

You are now shown the System

System

Properties dialog box. Its General tab displays your computer's operating system type, processor type, and amount of RAM.

> System:
>   Microsoft Windows 98
>   Second Edition
>   4.10.2222 A
>
> Registered to:
>   Gateway Evaluation System
>   34099-OEM-0080085-81279
>
>   Gateway EMEA
>   Gateway System
>   GenuineIntel
>   Pentium(r) III Processor
>   64.0MB RAM

Online help

Windows offers a searchable online help system:

- The 'help' means that the information is there to help you understand and use the operating system.

- The 'online' means that the material is presented on the computer screen rather than as a traditional printed manual.

You can search through and read online help by choosing **Start | Help**. Alternatively, when using My Computer or the Control Panel, choose **Help | Help Topics**.

You can search through and read online help in two ways: from the Help menu, or from dialog boxes.

Using Help menu options

Choose **Help | Contents and Index** to display the three tabs of the Help Topics dialog box. These are explained as follows:

Contents tab	*Index tab*	*Search tab*
This offers short descriptions of Windows 98's main features.	*Type the word or phrase you are interested in. In the lower-left of the dialog box, select a relevant item and click Display. In the pop-up box displayed, double-click on a topic. Windows shows help text in the right pane of the dialog box.*	*Type your question in the box at the top-left of the dialog box, and click List Topics. Windows displays a list of suggested help topics in the lower-left of the dialog box. Select a topic and click Display to view help text in the right pane.*
Where you see a heading with a book symbol, double-click to view the related sub-headings.		
Double-click on a question mark symbol to read the online help text.		

As you search through and read online help topics, you will see the following buttons at the top of the online help window:

- **Hide/Show**: Hides or displays the left pane of the online help dialog box.

- **Back/Forward**: Moves you backwards and forwards through previously visited help topics.

- **Print**: Prints the currently displayed help topic.

- **Options**: Offers a number of display choices.

Take a few minutes to look through the Windows online help system. Remember that you are free to use online help during an ECDL test.

Using help from dialog boxes

You can also access online help directly from a dialog box, as Exercise 2.4 demonstrates.

Exercise 2.4: Using online help in a dialog box

1 Choose **Start** | **Find** | **Files** or **Folders** to display the Find dialog box.

2 On the Name & Location tab, click in the Containing text: box.

3 Press F1. Windows displays online help text telling you about the purpose of the selected box.

> Provides a place for you to type some of the text contained in a file. If you don't know the file name, you may be able to find the file by typing some of its contents.

4 Click anywhere on the Find dialog box to remove the online help text.

Practise this exercise with other dialog boxes in Windows.

Chapter summary: so now you know

A *file* is the computer's basic unit of information storage. A *folder* is a group of files (and perhaps subfolders too). Grouping files into folders makes them easier to find and work with.

A *drive* is a physical storage device for holding files and folders. Typically, A: is the floppy drive, C: the hard disk, and D: is the CD-ROM drive.

Use *My Computer* to view the hierarchy of folders on your computer, and to see all the files and subfolders in any selected folder.

To display the details of a drive, folder or file, right-click on it and select the *Properties* option.

Windows adds a three-letter *file name extension* to every file, to indicate the file type. A full stop (.) separates the extension from the remainder of the file name. Common file name extensions are *.doc* (Word), *.xls* (Excel), *.mdb* (Access), and *.ppt* (PowerPoint).

To find a file on a drive, choose the **Start | Find | Files or Folders** command. Windows allows you to use *wildcards* to represent missing letters. You can also restrict your search to files of a certain date or date range, or that contain the specified keywords.

The Windows *online help* system provides a comprehensive and searchable guide to the system's features and procedures.

CHAPTER 3

Working with folders and files

In this chapter

In the previous chapter, you used My Computer to explore the folders and files on your PC. Now, you will learn how to perform actions on folders and files – how to create, name and rename, move and copy, and delete and undelete them – using the Windows Explorer application.

New skills

At the end of this chapter you should be able to:
- Create, save, rename, and delete folders
- Create, save, rename, and delete files
- Move and copy folders and files
- Select several folders or files, whether adjacent or non-adjacent

New words

At the end of this chapter you should be able to explain the
following terms:
- Windows Explorer
- Clipboard
- Pull-down menu
- Toolbar

About Windows Explorer

Think of a Windows application and names such as Word, Excel, and PowerPoint are probably the first to come to mind. But included with the Windows operating system is another, powerful application. It's called Windows Explorer and you can use it to:

- View the folders on your computer, and the hierarchy of sub-folders and files within any folder.

- Perform operations on various folders and files, such as renaming, copying, moving, and deleting.

You can open Windows Explorer in either of two ways:

- Choose **Start | Programs | Windows Explorer**, or

- Right-click on the **Start** button, and click **Explore**.

The two panes of Windows Explorer

Windows Explorer differs from My Computer in that its window is divided into left and right subwindows called panes.

- You use the *left pane* to select a particular drive or folder. You cannot view files in the left pane.

- You use the *right pane* to view the folders and files in the drive or folder selected in the left pane.

Toolbar ———→

Disk drives ⌈———→

Status Bar ———→

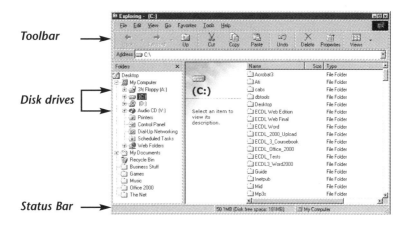

In the Windows Explorer left pane, you can see a hierarchical diagram of your computer's storage space:

- **Top level**: The Windows desktop.

- **Second level**: System folders such as My Computer and Recycle Bin, and any user-created desktop folders.

- **Third level**: Disk drives, control panel, and printers.

The right pane looks and works in a similar way to My Computer.

- Click on any drive in the left pane to display, in the right pane, the folders, and files stored on that drive.

- Double-click on any folder in the right pane to view any sub-folders and files contained within that folder.

Windows Explorer

A Windows application for viewing the hierarchy of folders and files, and for performing such actions as renaming, moving, and deleting.

Viewing options

As with My Computer, Windows Explorer offers a number of options that let you control how you view your drives, folders and files. Choose **View | Details** – it's the option that provides the most information in the smallest screen space.

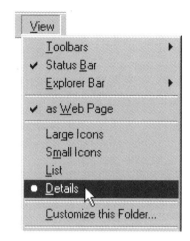

Along the bottom of the Windows Explorer window, in the Status Bar, you can see the number of items in the currently open folder (the one whose contents are shown in the right pane), the disk space occupied by the folder's contents, and the remaining free space on the drive.

If you can't see the Status Bar or the Toolbar, click the relevant options on the View menu to display them.

Follow Exercise 3.1 to practise your Windows Explorer skills.

Exercise 3.1: Viewing the Windows Folder

1 If Windows Explorer is not already open, open it now.

2 In the left pane, click on the C: drive icon.

3 In the right pane, scroll down until you see the Windows folder. Double-click on it.

   You can now see the folders and files stored within it. Folders are listed first. Scroll down through the Windows folder to see what files are within it.

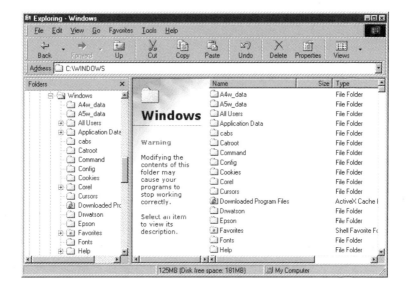

Explorer's plus and minus signs

In Windows Explorer, a folder without a plus (+) or a minus (-) sign in front of it is either empty or has only files inside it.

A folder with a plus (+) sign has folders inside it, and perhaps files too. To open it, click on the folder name or the + sign.

A minus (-) sign in front of a folder indicates that the folder is open – its sub-folders and files are currently displayed on the screen.

Click on a plus sign to display ('expand') or a minus sign to hide ('collapse') your view of a folder.

Working with folders

In the next few exercises you will use Windows Explorer to create folders and sub-folders, and to rename, delete and restore (undelete) folders.

Exercise 3.2: Creating two new folders

1 In the left pane of the Windows Explorer window, click on the C: drive.

2 Choose **File | New | Folder**. Windows displays a new folder at the bottom of the list in the right pane. It gives it the default name of 'New Folder'.

3 Type a name for your new folder. If your initials are KB, for example, call it KB Folder 1.

4 Repeat steps 1, 2, and 3. Name your second folder (say) KB Folder 2.

Exercise 3.3: Creating a sub-folder

1 In the right pane of the Windows Explorer window, double-click on the first folder that you created in Exercise 3.2 – in this example, the folder named KB Folder 1.

2 Choose **File | New | Folder**. Windows displays a new sub-folder.

3 Type a name for your new folder. If your initials are KB, for example, call it KB SubFolder 1.

Changing a folder's name

You can change a folder's name at any stage. Exercise 3.4 shows you how.

Exercise 3.4: Changing a folder's name

1   Right-click on one of your new folders to display a pop-up menu.

2   Choose **Rename**.

3   Type a new folder name. For example, KB New Folder.

     Well done! You have given your folder a new name.

Deleting a folder

Suppose that you don't need a folder any more – here's how to delete an unwanted folder:

Exercise 3.5: Deleting a folder

1   In the left pane of the Windows Explorer window, click on the first folder that you created in Exercise 3.2. It should contain the sub-folder you created in Exercise 3.3.

Delete button

2   In the left pane of the Windows Explorer window, right-click on the sub-folder. From the pop-up menu, select Delete.

     Alternatively, click once on the sub-folder to select it, and click the Delete button on the Windows Explorer Toolbar.

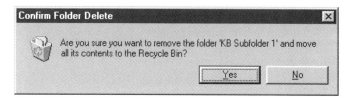

3   Click **Yes** to confirm that you want to remove the folder.

The folder is deleted, as are any sub-folders and files it may have contained.

Restoring a folder's files

Where did your deleted folder go? If it contained no files or folders, it has been deleted permanently by Windows. If it contained files or folders, Windows moves the files to the Recycle Bin. Follow the steps in Exercise 3.6 to bring your deleted folder and files back to life.

Exercise 3.6: Restoring a folder's files

1   In the left pane of the Windows Explorer window, scroll down until you can see the Recycle Bin, and click on it.

Windows Explorer now displays the contents of the Recycle Bin in the right pane.

2   Choose **Edit | Undo Delete** to restore the files and the folder that contained them.

Working with files

A file, as you learnt in Chapter 2, is the basic unit of information storage on a computer. In the next few exercises you will discover how to create, save and name, delete and restore a file.

Creating a file

Files are created by applications. For example, you can create a letter in Microsoft Word and a spreadsheet in Microsoft Excel.

The simplest type of file that you can create on a computer is a plain text file. A file of this kind contains just words, numbers and punctuation marks – and no fancy formatting or graphics of any kind.

The Windows application for creating plain text files is called Notepad.

Exercise 3.7: Creating a file

1   Choose **Start | Programs | Accessories | Notepad**. A blank Notepad window appears on your screen, ready to accept text.

2   Type the following words: Just testing

You have now created a file and entered content in that file. But your file is not saved on your hard disk. It exists only in the computer's memory. If the computer were to switch off for any reason, your file would be lost.

Naming and saving a file

The first time that you save a file, Windows asks you to give that file a name. Follow the steps in Exercise 3.8 to discover how.

Exercise 3.8: Naming and saving a file

1 Choose **File | Save** to view the Save As dialog box. By displaying this dialog box, Windows is asking:

   • What drive do you want to save your folder in?

   • What folder (or sub-folder) do you want to save your file in?

   • What name do you want to give your new file?

2 Click on the arrow at the right of the Save in: drop-down list box.

   Now, scroll up until you see the C: drive icon. Click on it.

   The Save As dialog box now displays a list of the folders on your C: drive.

3 Locate the folder that you renamed in Exercise 3.4. Double-click on it.

You have now told Windows the drive and folder where you want to save your file. All that remains is for you to give your new file a name.

4 Click in the File name: box, delete any text there, and type a name for your new file. If your initials are KB, for example, name it KB New File.

When finished, click Save.

Windows automatically adds the three-letter file name extension of .txt to all plain-text files created with the Notepad application.

Well done! You have learnt how to name and save a file.

Move the mouse to the top-right of the Notepad window, and click on the close box to close it.

Changing a file's name

You can change a file's name at any stage. Exercise 3.9 shows you how.

Exercise 3.9: Changing a file's name

1 Using Windows Explorer, open the folder containing the file you saved in Exercise 3.8.

2 Right-click on the file to display a pop-up menu.

3 Choose **Rename**.

4 Type a new file name. For example, KB Renamed File. Do not change or delete the file name extension (.txt).

Name	Size	Type
≣ KB Renamed File.txt	1KB	Text Document

You have given your file a new name. Another exercise completed!

Deleting a file

When you have been working on your computer for a while, you may find that its hard disk is taken up by files and folders you no longer use or need.

You can delete these files, but be careful not to delete any files that your computer needs to run programs! If in doubt, don't delete!

Exercise 3.10 shows you how to delete an unwanted file.

Exercise 3.10: Deleting a file

1 Using Windows Explorer, display and right-click on the file that you renamed in Exercise 3.9.

2 From the pop-up menu, select the **Delete** command.

3 Click **Yes** to confirm that you want to remove the file to the Recycle Bin.

Alternatively, click once on the file in Windows Explorer, and click the **Delete** button on the Toolbar.

Restoring a file

Follow the steps in Exercise 3.11 to restore your deleted file.

Exercise 3.11: Restoring a file

1   In the left pane of the Windows Explorer window, scroll until you can see the Recycle Bin, and click on it.

    Windows Explorer now displays the contents of the Recycle Bin in the right pane.

2   Click the file to select it, and then choose **File | Restore**.

The Windows clipboard

Suppose you want to place a folder or file in a different location on your computer. Or reproduce a folder or file so that two copies of it appear in different locations. Can you do it? Yes. This is a two-step process:

*   **Copy**: You select and then copy the folder or file to the clipboard, a temporary storage area. The selected folder or file remains in its original location.

    – or –

*   **Cut**: You select and then cut the folder or file to the clipboard. The selected folder or file is no longer in its original location.

*   **Paste**: You paste the folder or file from the clipboard into a different part of your computer – into a different folder, or even a different drive.

Clipboard

A temporary storage area to which you can copy or cut folders or files. You can paste from the clipboard to any location within the same or a different drive.

About the clipboard

Three points you should remember about the Windows clipboard:

- The clipboard is temporary. Turn off your computer and the clipboard contents are deleted.

- The clipboard can hold only a single, copied item at a time. If you copy or cut a second item, the second overwrites the first.

- Items stay in the clipboard after you paste from it, so you can paste the same folder or file into as many locations as you need.

Copying and moving folders

To copy a folder means to make a copy of it, and to place that copy in a new location. Exercise 3.12 takes you through the steps.

Exercise 3.12: Copying a folder

1   In the left pane of Windows Explorer, click the folder that you renamed in Exercise 3.4.

2   Choose **Edit | Copy** or click the Copy button on the Windows Explorer Toolbar.

Copy button

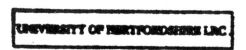

3   Scroll down the left pane until you can see the
Windows folder. Click on it to display its
contents in the right pane.

Paste button

4   Choose **Edit** | **Paste** or click the Paste
button on the Toolbar.

This places a copy of your folder within the Windows folder.

To move a folder means to place it in a new location – and
to remove it from its original location. Exercise 3.13 shows
you how.

Exercise 3.13: Moving a Folder

1   In the right pane, display the folder that you copied to the
Windows folder in Exercise 3.12. Click on it to select it.

2   Choose **Edit** | **Cut** or click the Cut button on
the Toolbar.

3   Scroll back up the right pane to locate the
folder named System.

Cut button

4   Double-click on the System folder to open it.

5   Choose **Edit** | **Paste** or click the Paste button on
the Toolbar.

This places your folder within the System folder of the
Windows folder.

Copying and moving files

In Exercise 3.14 you will make a copy of your plain-text file,
and place that copy in a different folder on your hard disk.
Following that, in Exercise 3.15, you will move the file from
its current folder to a new one.

Exercise 3.14: Copying a File

1 In the left pane, display the folder containing the file that you created in Exercise 3.7. Double-click on the folder to display its contents in the right pane.

2 Choose **Edit | Copy** or click the Copy button on the Toolbar.

3 In the left pane, scroll down to locate the folder called Windows.

4 Click on the Windows folder to open it. Its contents are now listed in the right pane.

5 Choose **Edit | Paste** or click the Paste button on the Toolbar.

You have now placed a copy of your file within the Windows folder.

Exercise 3.15: Moving a File

1 In the right pane, display the file that you copied to the Windows folder in Exercise 3.14. Click on it to select it.

2 Choose **Edit | Cut** or click the Cut button on the Toolbar.

3 Scroll back up the right pane to locate the folder named System.

4 Double-click the System folder to open it.

5 Choose **Edit | Paste** or click the Paste button on the Toolbar.

You have now moved the file to the System sub-folder of the Windows folder.

Working with multiple files

Windows Explorer provides an easy method of copying or
moving several files in a single operation. This method works
only when:

- The files you want to copy or move are currently
  located in the *same* folder.

- The place you want to copy or move them to is also a
  single folder.

When you list the files to copy or move in Windows Explorer,
two situations are possible:

- The files are *adjacent*. They are positioned immediately
  below or above one another.

- The files are *non-adjacent*. They are not positioned
  immediately below or above one another.

If the files are adjacent, follow these steps:

- Click on the first file

- Press and hold down the Shift key

- Click on the last file

All the files – the first, last, and in-between –
are now selected, and you can copy or cut
them in a single operation.

If the files are non-adjacent, follow these steps:

- Click on the first file

- Press and hold down the Ctrl key

- Click the relevant files, one after the other, to select them.

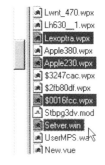

Again, all the files are now selected, and you can copy or cut them in a single operation.

When selecting several files, you can scroll down or up as you make your selection. This methods works for folders as well as files. Another operation that you can perform on selected folders or files is deletion. Simply select the adjacent or non-adjacent files or folders, and click the Delete button on the Toolbar.

Menu bars, toolbars and shortcuts

In the final part of this chapter, you will discover the three ways that you perform actions in a Windows application: menu commands, toolbar buttons, and keyboard shortcuts.

Menu bars

Start the Microsoft Word application. Take a look at the line of words that runs just under the title bar. Each of these words represents a pull-down menu.

Word's menu bar ──➤   File Edit View Insert Format Tools Data Window Help

Click the **File** menu name to display the commands (actions) available on this menu. You tell Word that you want to perform a particular action by clicking the action's name on the pull-down menu. Click the **Exit** command to close Word.

Pull-down

A list of options that appears when you click on a menu name. The menu name is generally on a menu bar along the top of the window, and the menu appears below that bar, as if you pulled it down.

Whenever you see an arrow to the right of a menu option, selecting that option displays a further submenu of choices.

All Windows applications share a number of common menus. Understand their general purpose and you will be able to use most applications. The common menus are:

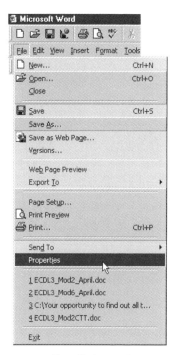

Word's pull-down File menu

• **File**: Use the commands on this menu to create a new (blank) file, open an existing file, save the current file, save the current file with a new name (**Save as**), print the current file, and quit the application.

- **Edit**: Use the commands on this menu to copy and move selected files, or items (such as text or graphics) within files.

- **View**: Use the commands on this menu to display your file in different ways, including a zoomed-in (close up) view or zoomed out (bird's eye) view.

- **Help**: Use the commands on this menu to display online help information about the application you are using.

Toolbars

A second way of performing an action is to click a button on a toolbar. Instead of choosing **File | Save** to save a file, for example, you could click the Save button on the toolbar. Not every menu command has a toolbar button equivalent, but the most commonly used commands do.

Toolbar

A collection of buttons that you can click to perform frequently used actions, such as creating, opening, or saving files, and for clipboard operations.

Here are the toolbar buttons that you will find on almost every Windows application:

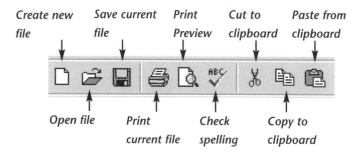

Keyboard shortcuts

A third way of performing actions in
Windows is to use keyboard shortcuts.
You may find using these faster than
either menu commands or toolbar
buttons, as you need not take either
hand away from the keyboard.

Keyboard shortcut for
copying a selected
item to the clipboard

An example of a keyboard shortcut is Ctrl+c, which means
'Hold down the control key and press the letter c key'. This
has the same effect as choosing **Edit | Copy** or clicking the
Copy button on the toolbar.

Here are the most commonly used shortcut keys:

Keyboard Shortcut	Action Performed	Menu Command
Ctrl+o	Opens an existing file	File | Open
Ctrl+n	Opens a new file	File | New
Ctrl+s	Saves the current file	File | Save
Ctrl+c	Copies to the clipboard	Edit | Copy
Ctrl+x	Cuts to the clipboard	Edit | Cut
Ctrl+v	Pastes from the clipboard	Edit | Paste

Chapter summary: so now you know

Use *Windows Explorer* to view the hierarchy of folders on your
computer, and to view and work with the drives, folders and
files on your computer. Windows Explorer displays two
subwindows or panes. You use the *left pane* to select a
particular drive or folder. You use the *right pane* to view the
folders and files in the drive or folder selected in the left pane.

Windows Explorer enables you to *copy, move, rename,* and *delete* folders and files. You can also create folders with Windows Explorer. You create files with software applications. The *clipboard* is a temporary storage area to which you can copy or cut folders or files. You can paste from the clipboard to any location within the same or a different drive.

You can *select multiple files,* and then copy, cut, paste, or delete them in a single operation. If the files are *adjacent,* click the first file, hold down the Shift key, and then click the last file. If non-adjacent, click the first file, hold down the Ctrl key, and then click the individual files to select them.

A *pull-down* menu is a list of options that appears when you click a menu name on a menu bar. When you see an arrow to the right of a menu option, selecting that option displays a further *submenu* of choices. You tell Word that you want to perform a particular action by clicking the action's name on the pull-down menu.

A second way of performing an action is to click a button on a toolbar. Most applications have toolbar buttons for creating, opening, or saving files, and for clipboard operations.

A third option is to press the Ctrl key in combination with a particular letter key. Examples of such *keyboard shortcuts* include Ctrl+c to copy to the clipboard and Ctrl+v to paste from it.

CHAPTER 4

Mastering Windows

In this chapter

Now that you are familiar with Windows basics, you are ready to move on to the more advanced features.

You will discover how to take control of your Windows desktop, enabling you to customize it to reflect your working needs and your personal taste. You will also learn how to make back-up copies of your files on diskettes.

New skills

At the end of this chapter you should be able to:

- Personalize your desktop by moving icons and creating folders to hold application and file icons
- Create shortcuts that take you directly to a particular application, file or folder
- Select a screen saver

- Customize your wallpaper, scheme and screen resolution
- Change your computer's date and time settings
- Adjust your computer's sound volume
- Change your computer's regional settings
- Format a diskette
- Copy a file to a diskette
- Save a file to a diskette
- Use various print features and options

New words

At the end of this chapter you should be able to explain the following terms:
- Desktop shortcut
- Screen saver
- Print queue

Managing your desktop

You can arrange your Windows desktop to suit your working needs and personal taste:

- To reposition your icons, simply drag them to where you want them.

- To make your screen look tidier, create desktop folders and place application and file icons in them.

You create a desktop folder as follows:

- Right-click on the desktop to display a pop-up menu.

- Choose **New | Folder**. Windows creates a desktop folder with the default name New Folder.

- Type your folder name, and press Enter.

Next, double-click the folder to open it, and drag icons into it, either from the desktop or from other desktop folders.

Creating desktop shortcuts

You will use some applications more frequently than others. You can save yourself time by creating a shortcut to these programs from your desktop (or from a folder on your desktop). As a result, you won't have to go the **Start | Programs** route every time you want to start that application.

Follow the steps in Exercise 4.1 to create a desktop shortcut for Notepad.

Exercise 4.1: Creating a desktop shortcut for Notepad

1   Chose **Start | Programs | Windows Explorer**. If the Explorer window occupies the full Windows desktop, click on the restore button (top-right).

2   Display the application for which you want to create a shortcut. You will find Notepad in the Windows folder.

Name	Size	Type	Modified	
Notepad.exe	62KB	Application	23/04/99 22:22	
notify.dat	1KB	DAT File	17/02/01 17:14	
NPSExec.exe	43KB	Application	02/04/99 16:37	

3   Right-click on the Notepad icon, drag it from Windows Explorer onto your desktop, and release the right mouse button.

Shortcut to
Notepad.exe

If you don't like your shortcut's default name, right-click on it, choose **Rename**, type a new name, and press the Enter key.

You can also create shortcuts for frequently used folders and files. You can leave the Notepad icon on your desktop, or drag it to a desktop folder.

Desktop shortcut

A user-created icon that, when clicked on, takes you directly to an application, folder or file. It is a fast, convenient alternative to using the Start menu.

In Exercise 4.2 you will create a desktop folder named Office 2000, and create desktop shortcuts for four Office applications within it.

Exercise 4.2: Creating an Office 2000 desktop folder containing shortcuts

1 Right-click on your desktop. On the pop-up menu displayed, choose **New | Folder**. Windows creates a folder with the default name New Folder.

2 Type the following folder name Office 2000, and press Enter.

3 Double-click your new folder to open it. You are now ready to create desktop shortcuts and place them within the folder.

4 Let's start with a shortcut to Microsoft Word. Choose **Start | Find | Files or Folders** to display the Find dialog box.

5 In the Named: box, type Winword.exe, and click **Find Now**.

6 When Winword.exe is found, right-click on its icon, and drag it from the Find dialog box into your Office 2000 desktop folder.

7 Click on the Find dialog box again. Repeat steps 5 and 6 for the following other Office 2000 application files: Excel.exe, Powerpnt.exe and Msaccess.exe.

When finished, you may wish to rename the shortcut icons as shown.

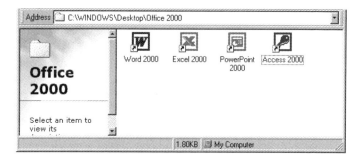

You can now close the new Office 2000 desktop folder.

Setting the time and date

Is your computer set to the correct date and time? If not, the files you create and edit, and e-mails you send, will show misleading dates or times. Exercise 4.3 shows you how to set the date and time on your computer.

Date/Time

Exercise 4.3: Setting your computer's date and time

1 Choose **Start | Settings | Control Panel**.

2 On the folder displayed, double-click the Date/Time icon.

3 Make the changes you want. Click **Apply** and then **OK**.

A small battery inside your computer ensures that Windows remembers the date and time settings, even when your computer is turned off.

Adjusting the sound volume

Modern PCs have the ability to play sound files through attached loudspeakers or headphones. Follow Exercise 4.4 to discover how to adjust the playback volume setting on your computer.

Exercise 4.4: Changing the playback volume

1   Click the Volume Control icon displayed towards the right of the taskbar. The icon's appearance depends on the type of sound card installed on your computer. Typically, it looks like a small loudspeaker.

    If you are unsure which taskbar icon is the Volume Control, position the cursor over each icon until you see a text box telling you the icon's purpose.

2   On the pop-up menu shown, drag the Volume Control slider up to raise the volume or down to lower it.

    You can switch off sound completely by selecting the Mute box.

3   When finished, click on any other part of your screen to close the Volume Control.

Setting the screen saver

A screen saver is a program that takes over the computer's display screen if there are no keystrokes or mouse movements for a specified amount of time.

They were developed originally to prevent damage to monitors that could arise if one fixed image was displayed continuously over a long period – such as a weekend, for example. Screen savers prevent this, either by blanking out the screen entirely or by displaying a series of constantly moving images.

Today's monitors are less likely to suffer from the problem that screen savers were designed to prevent, and they are now mostly an adornment.

Exercise 4.5 shows you how to set up or change your computer's screen saver.

Screen Saver

> *A program that takes over the computer's display screen if there are no keystrokes or mouse movements for a specified amount of time. They either blank out the screen entirely or display a series of continually moving images.*

Exercise 4.5: Setting up or changing your screen saver

1   Right-click on the Windows desktop, choose **Properties** from the pop-up menu, and select the **Screen Saver** tab.

2   Click the arrow to the right of the Screen Saver drop-down list box to display a list of screen savers installed on your computer.

3 Click to select the screen saver you require from the list.

4 In the Wait: box type the number of minutes before which the screen saver will activate, and click **OK**.

To clear the screen saver after it has started, move your mouse or press any key.

Customizing your screen

The appearance of Windows on your computer is controlled by the setting of the following two items, each of which you can change to suit your working needs or personal taste:

- Wallpaper

- Scheme

Wallpaper

You can insert an image, such as a scanned photograph or a picture downloaded from the internet, on your desktop background. Follow these steps to do so:

- Right-click on the desktop, choose **Properties** from the pop-up menu, and select the Background tab.

- Select your required wallpaper from the list box.

- Select Center to position the image in the middle of your desktop, or Tile to repeat the image horizontally and vertically until it fills the entire screen, and click **OK**.

Scheme

This is the combination of colours, fonts, and spacing that controls the appearance of such items as title bars, scroll bars, and icons. To view or adjust your scheme:

- Right-click on the desktop, choose **Properties** from the pop-up menu, and select the Appearance tab.

- Select your required scheme from the Scheme drop-down list box, and click **OK**.

You can change your wallpaper and scheme as often as you wish. The relevant dialog boxes offer a preview area where you can view the effect of any changes before you apply them. Don't be afraid to experiment with different settings.

Changing your screen resolution

Everything you view on your screen is composed of tiny square dots called pixels. The number of pixels displayed is determined by your screen resolution.

- Lower resolution settings (such as 640×480) result in fewer, larger pixels, so that everything on your screen appears bigger and blockier.

- Higher resolution settings (such as 1024×768) use more, smaller pixels, so that everything appears smaller and more defined.

To change your screen resolution:

- Right-click on the desktop, choose **Properties** from the pop-up menu, and select the Settings tab.

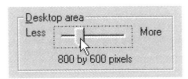

- Drag the Desktop area slider left to decrease the resolution or right to increase it.

You can see the effect of a new screen resolution in the preview area. When finished, click **OK** to save your new settings and close the dialog box.

Changing your regional settings

The options you select in the Windows Regional Settings decide the default currency symbol shown in your applications, and which conventions Windows uses when displaying times, dates, and numbers.

To change your regional settings:

Regional Settings

- Choose **Start | Settings | Control Panel**, and click the Regional Settings icon.

- On the Regional Settings tab, select the relevant region from the drop-down list.

- To override the default conventions for your selected region, use the options on the Number, Currency, Time, and Date tabs.

- When finished, click **OK** to save your new settings and to close the dialog box.

Working with diskettes

You can copy files and folders from your hard disk to a floppy diskette to:

- Make a copy of your work that you can give to a colleague or friend.

- Have a second, backup copy of your work just in case your computer is somehow damaged and the files on it are 'lost'.

The more regularly you make backups, the more up to date your files will be if your computer fails.

Formatting a diskette

You can only copy files to a diskette that is formatted. When Windows formats a floppy diskette, it:

- Sets up a 'table of contents' on the diskette which it later uses to locate files stored on the disk.

- Checks for any damaged areas, and, when it finds them, marks those areas as off-limits for file storage.

Most new diskettes come already formatted. But it is cheaper to buy unformatted ones and format them yourself. The ECDL Syllabus also specifies that you must know how to format a diskette. Exercise 4.6 shows you how.

Exercise 4.6: Formatting a floppy diskette

1 Insert the floppy diskette you want to format into the diskette drive.

2 Chose **Start | Programs | Windows Explorer** and right-click the A: drive icon in the left-hand pane.

3 Choose **Format** and select the following two options on the dialog box displayed:

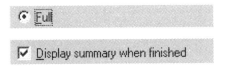

4 When Windows has formatted the disk, click OK to display the Format Results dialog box.

5 Click **Close**.

Formatting a disk overwrites any table of contents there may have been previously on the disk, so making it impossible for Windows to find files that were saved on the diskette before it was formatted.

For that reason, don't even think about formatting your computer's hard disk.

You cannot format a disk if there are files open on that disk.

Copying a file to a diskette

You can copy a file to a diskette using the copy-and-paste option available with Windows Explorer. See Exercise 4.7.

Exercise 4.7: Copying a file to a diskette

1   Place a formatted diskette in the A: drive of your computer.

2   Choose **Start | Programs | Windows Explorer** and, in the right-hand pane, display the file that you want to copy – for example, the Mouse.txt file from the Windows folder.

License.txt	32KB	Text Document	23/04/99 22:22
Modemdet.txt	1KB	Text Document	11/12/99 14:39
Mouse.txt	6KB	Text Document	23/04/99 22:22
Msdosdrv.txt	45KB	Text Document	23/04/99 22:22
Ndislog.txt	0KB	Text Document	27/04/01 00:25

3   Click on the file and choose **Edit | Copy** or click the Copy button on the toolbar.

4   In the left pane, click on the A: drive icon.

If there are currently any files on the diskette, Windows Explorer lists them in its right pane.

5   Choose **Edit | Paste** or click the Paste button to copy the file to the diskette.

Saving a file to a diskette

A second way to copy a file to a diskette is to use the **File |
Save As** command of the application in which you created
and worked with the file. If you currently have the
application open on your screen, this is faster than using
Windows Explorer. See Exercise 4.8.

Exercise 4.8: Saving a file to a diskette

1 Choose **Start | Programs | Accessories** | Notepad.

2 Choose **File | Open**, locate the file you saved in Exercise
   2.32, and click **Open**.

3 Choose **File | Save As**, locate the A: drive, and click **Save**
   to save the file.

   A copy of the Notepad file is now stored on the diskette.

Printing files

Now that you can open and work with files, you will want to
print copies of your work so you can see it on paper.

Exercise 4.9: Printing a file

1 Open the file, for example, a Word document.

2 Select **File | Print**.

3 Click **OK** in the Print dialog box.

   If your printer is connected and set up correctly, your file
   should print.

The print queue

What happens to a file after you choose to print it with the Print command? It goes to a file called a print queue, and is then taken from the print queue by the selected printer.

The print queue can store a number of files, which the printer then collects in turn as it becomes ready to print them. The time it takes to print a file depends on the number and size of the other print jobs in the print queue.

You can view your print queue to see what print jobs are waiting in it, delete print jobs from the queue, and reorder the sequence in which print jobs are listed.

Print queue

> *A list of files (print jobs) that are waiting to be printed.*
> *The printer pulls the files off the queue one at a time.*

Viewing the print queue

What jobs are currently in the print queue? See Exercise 4.10 to find out.

Exercise 4.10: Viewing the print queue

1   Choose **Start | Settings | Printers**.

2   Double-click on the icon for the printer you want to check.

Windows displays a list of all the print jobs in the queue.

Cancelling a print job in the queue

There are many reasons why you may decide to cancel a print job – you may discover that the job is not printing correctly. You may realise that you already have a copy of the printout. Or you may simply change your mind about printing the file.

Follow the steps in Exercise 4.11 to cancel a job.

Exercise 4.11: Removing a job from the print queue

1 Choose **Start | Settings | Printers**.

2 Double-click on the icon for the printer you want to look at. Windows displays a list of all the print jobs in the queue.

3 Select the document you want to cancel printing.

4 Choose **Document | Cancel Printing**.

Changing the order of jobs in the print queue

You can change the current sequence of jobs in the print queue. Here's how.

Exercise 4.12: Reordering the jobs in the print queue

1 Choose **Start | Settings | Printers**.

2 Double-click on the icon for the printer you want to look at. Windows displays a list of all the print jobs in the queue.

3 Select the file you want to move, and drag it to the required place in the queue.

You can't move a file that is already printing.

Deleting all documents from the print queue

Follow the steps in Exercise 4.13 to remove all pending print jobs from the print queue.

Exercise 4.13: Deleting all jobs in the print queue

1 Choose **Start | Settings | Printers**.

2 Double-click on the icon for the printer you want to look at. Windows displays a list of all the print jobs in the queue.

3 Choose **Printer | Purge Jobs**.

The Print dialog box

When you choose the **File | Print** command within an application, you are shown a dialog box that typically offers the following options:

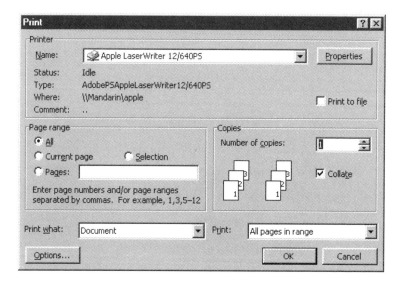

Name

To choose a different
printer, click on the
arrow on the right of the
Name: drop-down list

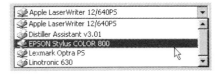

box, and then click the printer you require.

Print range

You can choose to print all pages, the currently displayed
page only or a range of pages.

　To print a group of continuous pages, enter the first and
last page number of the group, separated by a dash. For
example, 2–6 or 12–13.

　To print a non-continuous group of pages, enter their
individual page numbers, separated by commas. For example,
3, 5, 9 or 12, 17, 34. You can combine continuous with non-
continuous page selections.

Copies

You can specify how many copies of the file you want to print.
For multiple copies, ensure that the Collate checkbox is selected.

The Properties button

Clicking on the Properties
button displays some further
print choices that will vary
with the type of printer
selected – colour or black-
and-white, inkjet, or laser.

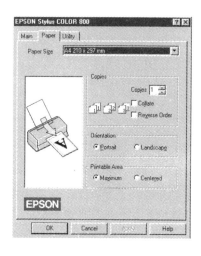

All printers offer choices
about paper size (A4 is
standard) and orientation
(Portrait means 'standing
up', Landscape means
'on its side').

When you have selected your options, click **OK** to print
your file.

Print Preview

Most Windows applications have a **Print Preview** command
on their **File** menu that lets you see on-screen how the file
contents will look when printed on paper.

Changing the default printer

If your PC is attached to a network, you may have a number
of printers available to you. It's a good idea to set the printer
you use most often as the default printer. When you choose
the **File | Print** command in Word or other Windows
applications, your file outputs on the default printer unless
you specify otherwise.

Follow this procedure to set a printer as the default printer:

- Choose **Start | Settings | Printers**.

- Right-click on the icon of
the printer you want to set as
the default.

- Select the **Set As Default**
command from the pop-up menu.

If there is a check mark beside this
command, the printer is already
selected as the default printer.

Chapter summary: so now you know

You can *personalize* your Windows desktop by repositioning
icons, creating new folders, and placing application and file
icons in them. You can create desktop *shortcuts* – icons that
take you directly to a particular application, file or folder.
You can also customize your *wallpaper, background pattern,
scheme,* and *screen saver*.

You can adjust the *date and time* settings on your
computer so that Windows attaches the correct date and
time to the files you create and edit, and to e-mails you
send. You can also adjust the *sound volume*.

By either blanking out the screen or showing a series of
continually moving images, a *screen saver* program takes
over the computer's display screen if there are no keystrokes
or mouse movements for a specified amount of time.

Your *Regional Settings* decide the default currency symbol shown in your applications, and which conventions Windows uses when displaying times, dates, and numbers.

Your *screen resolution* is the number of pixels it displays. Lower-resolution settings make everything appear bigger and blockier. Higher-resolution settings make everything appear smaller and more defined.

Before you can copy files to a floppy diskette, you must *format* the diskette. If you format a previously used diskette, any files that may have been on the disk are no longer accessible.

Anything you print goes first to a file called a *print queue* that can hold multiple print jobs. It is then taken from the print queue by the selected printer. You can view your print queue to see what jobs are waiting in it, delete jobs from the queue, and reorder the sequence in which jobs are listed.

You have now completed the final section of ECDL Module 2. Congratulations.